What Is Autism?

Author: Amy Senior
Illustrated by: Daniel Aiers

My name is Cole and I have autism.

What is autism you ask?

Here are the basics.

What Is Autism?

Autism is disorder that some children are born with or develop early in life. The doctors call it, autism spectrum disorder. Autism affects the brain and makes talking and playing with others very difficult.

Children with autism often have trouble with the following:

- Looking at you
- Talking to you
- Standing still
- Taking turns
- Rules
- Understanding how to play a game
- Understanding jokes

Some children with autism have special gifts and talents.
Like playing the drums or knowing everything there is to know about trains.

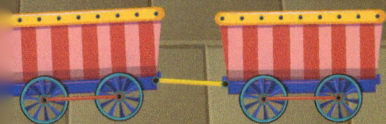

Some children with autism
can go to school just like you,
and some might have to attend
a special school.

Sometimes it can seem as if children with autism want to be left alone, or seem rude. That is because children with autism have a hard time playing with others and expressing their feelings.

Children with autism often do things that seem unusual like as the following:

- Saying the same word over and over
- Moving their arms or body in a certain ways
- Rocking or twirling
- Flapping their hands or spinning
- Lining up all of their toys in a straight line

When they do this, it's almost as if their brains have
a case of the hiccups.

Children with autism tend to have a harder time developing friendships. This might be because they have trouble with:
- Talking to other children
- Working out what other children are thinking and feeling
- Taking part in other children's activities
- Understanding facial expressions and body language
- Adjusting to new social situations
- Solving social problems, like how to sort out disagreements.

Children with autism might need help developing skills in these areas.

You can encourage friendships by asking them if they would like to be friends and if they would like to play. Ask them about their favorite movie or toy.

Children with autism want to have friends and have fun too. Sometimes their autism gets in the way of them making friends and playing with other children. They don't like it when others stare at them and their behaviors.
Children with autism want to be accepted for who they are and treated like other children.

What causes autism?

No one really knows what causes autism. It is highly researched and there are many opinions, but no scientific evidence on the exact cause.

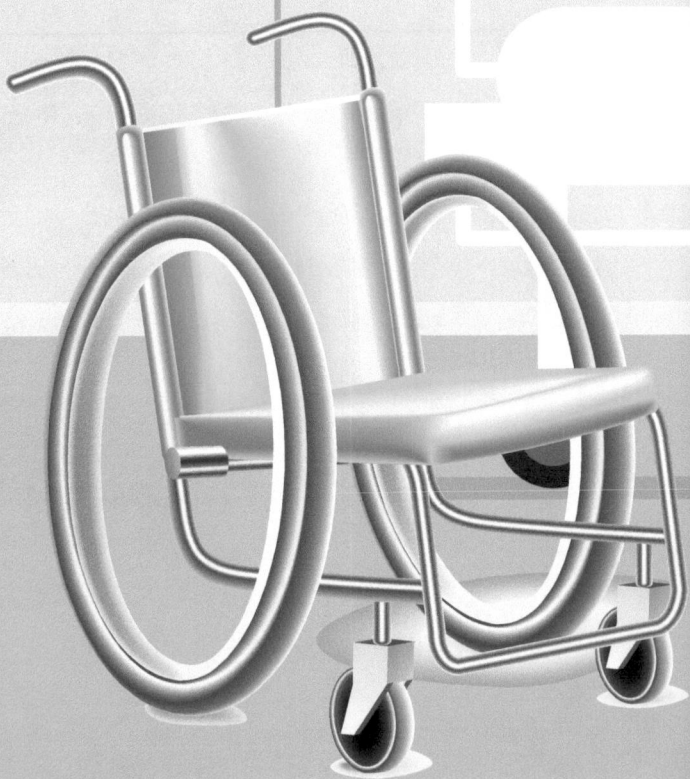

What is the treatment for autism?

Their are many different therapies that help with all of the issues children with autism deal with. But there is no cure for autism.

Children with autism may act differently than their peers. They want to be treated like other children their age and have the same opportunities.

Remember:

- They can't help some of their behaviors and actions.
- They have a hard time talking with others and expressing their feelings.
- They have a hard time understanding and following the rules.
- They have a hard time making friends and they want to be treated like other children their age.

That is what children with autism, like myself, deal with everyday.
So the next time you meet someone with autism, remember what you learned in this book!

In a culture that bombards us with messages that perfection is the key to happiness, autistic individuals and their families dare to challenge this notion while drawing others to look beneath and beyond the superficial.

Beneath and beyond autism there is reality often missed, a will, a soul, an identity in ways not seen or appreciated by surface observation.

www.ingramcontent.com/pod-product-compliance
Lightning Source LLC
Chambersburg PA
CBHW040347060426
42445CB00029B/29